Essence of the Burren

Essence of the Burren

A unique presentation on the Burren
in the West of Ireland
through the eyes of a holistic therapist
and geomancer.

The following books written by the author are available to purchase at
www.celtictrails.co.uk/books-for-sale-2/
www.earthwise.me
www.facebook.com/earthwiseconnect

- Spirit of the Burren
- The Lothians Unveiled
- The Culdees
- Rosslyn Chapel and Hinterland
- The Spiritual Meaning of Rosslyn's Carvings
- The Spiritual Purpose to Rosslyn
- Arks within Grail Lands
- Eternal Elements
- Tree Murmurs

First edition Autumn 2014
Copyright © 2014 Jackie Queally

The author reserves all rights to the content of this book. No part may be reproduced in any fashion without the express written permission of the author, with the exception of quotations embodied in critical articles.

Neither may it be stored in a retrieval system or transmitted in any form, or by any means, without the permission of the publisher.

Cover by:
Tina Robinson

Book interior layout and design by:
Danial Amen

Technical Support by:
Ruth Queally

Photos by:
Jackie Queally and Kevin Lynch

Proof Reading by:
Spruce Krier and Trish Kirby

Published by:
Earthwise Publications

Printed by:
Lightning Source

ISBN: 978-0-9930512-0-3

Essence of the Burren

Spirit of the Burren

Spirit of Burren is a branch of a small company EarthWise that offers guidance in planning tours of sacred sites, delivers talks and workshops on the wisdom of the Earth, creates workshops and retreats that assist you to reconnect with the divinity of the Earth, and also creates books such as these.

In our workshops that we call Gaia Journeys we use an array of modalities such as Gaia Touch (earth yoga exercises founded by Marko Pogacnik), sacred sound, and energy dowsing to deepen your inner and outer connection with Gaia, the name for the living Earth.

For further details see www.earthwise.me

or email jackiequeally@gmail.com in the first instance.

Essence of the Burren

CONTENTS

Introduction — 1

Chapter 1

Water — 09

Chapter 2

Wood — 17

Chapter 3

Fire — 25

Chapter 4

Earth — 33

Chapter 5

Metal — 41

Essence of the Burren

INTRODUCTION

Limestone pavement on Lough Avalla walk nearing dusk when natural pink hue appears on rocks.

The Burren is an area of bare limestone hills and lowlands in south Galway and north Clare in the west of Ireland. It is a unique geological region resurrected from deep tropical sea beds of long ago, and has gained status as an internationally recognized geo-park.

Underlain with deep granite beds, its intense beauty and other-worldly mood has struck deeply into many hearts. It is a challenge to describe the Burren adequately — the Burren is made of small egg-like grains of limestone known as oolitic limestone. It is said that the soft femininity of the rock is borne out in the softness of its inhabitants. That same soft quality that listens and nurtures is prevalent among the menfolk as much as the womenfolk here. I wanted for a long time to find my unique voice and apply it to the land of my ancestors. In the end, I looked to the East for inspiration.

Before revealing that inspiration, I must explain that I have always had a feel for the land in ways that were inwardly, rather than outwardly, sensed. When out on the land my thinking automatically slows down when I approach an area, sensing that the land is sentient and living: indeed Earth is a sentient being, functioning at a far more subtle level than many realise. Moreover there is a vital albeit subtle interaction between the Earth and humans. Ancient cultures understood that and their leaders treated the Earth with reverence, understanding that its natural commodities were gifts to be treated with respect, rather than exploitation. If Earth is to survive, we have to rekindle our inter-connection with Her.

The earth responds to love as much as we do. When people love and cherish nature they tend it well, and the land "sings" in response to their good custodianship. Within the Burren there are several places where caring farming practices have resulted in a healthy and positive two-way flow between farmers and the Earth. We can readily sense this as we pass through their land.

My inspiration began with a perception that the Earth and human beings are both forms of living temples, with layers of subtle energies that thrive when nurtured and respected. How can various locations on the Earth be presented so as to give justice to the vast and intricate range of qualities and energies they hold? Using the Burren as a wonderful backdrop, I decided to refer to a human energy system known as the Five Elements, used widely in the Far East. I first learnt about this energy system when training and practising as a sonic acupuncturist and masseuse. The classical oriental meridians or energy lines are the baseline. My tuning forks would activate the meridians to achieve balance and greater energy in the client's energy system. The meridians in the body are all contained within a universal, dynamic energy system known as the Five Elements. They are Water, Wood, Fire, Metal and Earth.

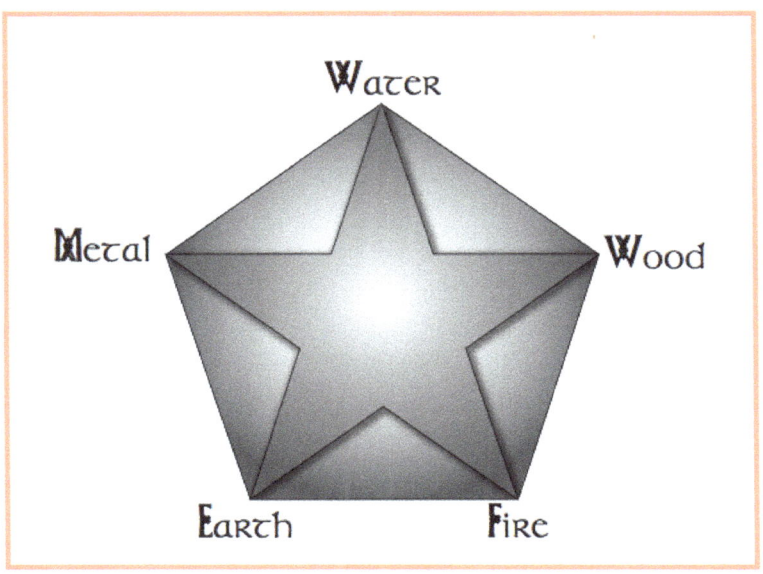

Introduction

Starting from the viewpoint then that the land is sentient, I sought to express the nature of the Burren. I decided to use the simple yet effective Five Element theory to reveal the rare qualities of the Burren landscape. Thus I had my skeleton upon which to hang my energetic sensing of the Burren!

What are these five elements and how do they work together?

There is a cycle of life to our being. The ancient Orientals divided the cycle into five main components based on the elements of Water, Wood, Fire, Metal and Earth. It is interesting that in the West we have a cyclical division into four — Earth, Air, Fire and Water. In the Orient they reserved space for a fifth element that is the ether which they called Metal, similar to our Air element. When I looked at the Five Elements I felt that Water element is best suited to introduce the Five Element cycle in Ireland, particularly in the Burren where so much water lies under the rocks.

Water is the source of life. Our planet mainly consists of water (and Ireland is an especially watery place): likewise our bodies mainly consist of water. Water feeds all vegetation which the Wood Element encompasses. Wood then feeds the element of Fire which in turn empowers the Earth, leaving minerals in its ashes. Consider how volcanoes yield rich soils. Finally the Earth feeds the element of Metal found in metallic seams within the Earth. This is an empowering cycle that has its psychological and spiritual counterparts.

Introduction

Departing from the wheel momentarily, in order to present the Burren in this energetic cycle I had to delve into what I already knew, and also what came to me in inspired moments. I knew my deep interest in an early Christian movement which did not follow the Roman style of Christianity had to play a significant role, as these pioneering spirits inhabited the wild and lonely places of the Burren to a greater extent than elsewhere in Ireland, and left their tangible presence and mark on the Burren landscape.

I am referring here to the Culdees, whom many have gleaned held deep mystical knowledge that bridged Heaven and Earth. (1) Historians and intuitives alike have been attracted to knowing more about this group, and in recent years more has been written on this strictly oral tradition. Some years ago I had professional dealings with Fiontullach, the leader of the modern day Culdees, who go by their ancient name Ceile De. They faithfully continue a lineage of strictly oral traditions that honour the pure Christ state of being, which they perceive as present in nature, in both male and female forms. Through ancient chants and prayers they expound the beauty of their once secret knowledge — a knowledge that holds echoes of what I sensed for many years had driven the early Christians to live in the Burren. According to mystics, the Culdees of the past understood deep Druidic mysteries of the inner Earth, as well as the cosmic mysteries of the stars. They were able to perform certain white magic, and understood principles and codings of sacred geometry that climaxed in the later carpet pages of missals . They walked a good deal, and understood how to utilize the natural variations in energetic frequencies in the Earth in order to draw closer to their Creator. I know that invisible lines of high energies that lay across the land were recognised, utilized or even installed by the Culdees in parts of Scotland, and I discovered that many of their hermitages here in the Burren were likewise placed on significant leylines.

These energy lines in the land often connected one powerful gathering site or special nature site to another. You can create a leyline by love and intent. This is an ancient art that some cultures who survive from older times still deploy. For a longer explanation of ley lines read my longer book on the region. (2)

This increase in 'earth energy' along leylines, or even on vortex spots, reflects changes in electromagnetism that some pioneering scientists have been measuring in recent decades. I discovered that slight alterations in the rock type help create a burst of subtle energy too. Writers such as Freddy Silva (3) who study the construction of sacred temples have explained very convincingly how the shape and the positioning of buildings affect the Earth's subtle energy forces in order to assist in raising the consciousness of devotees.

In the past our architects used to work with esoteric knowledge when they studied the effects of music and geometry upon man's mood. In the Burren, the simple rectangular cell churches that you can find in isolated places bore the Golden Mean proportion in their dimensions (1: 1.618). The Golden Mean was used a good deal in the Middle Ages by architects and painters to impart a quality of harmony in their creations. They believed it created a link between Heaven and Earth, as the mathematical ratio occurs in many natural phenomena. Here in the Burren the simple cell churches were constructed so that the length and breadth of the walls adhered to the "Golden Mean rectangle" the effect of which was believed to raise the vibration of the hermetic, and thus aid him or her commune with the less dense, divine levels they sought.

Soon we will look closer at Water, the first element in our cycle. After that the wheel naturally turns to Wood, which indeed fits the personality of the aforementioned early Christians, for the psychological traits of the Wood Element epitomise pioneer thinking. The early settler monks of both sexes were indeed pioneers of faith, and lived hermetic lives in harmony with nature. They did not concern themselves with external affairs, seeming keen instead on developing inner strengths. Interestingly archaeologists point out that the Burren had not been used by early settlers enmasse for ritual ceremonies, with perhaps one exception located in the East, at the very extremity between the lowlands and the higher hills (this is Turlough Hill, a "liminal landscape" with its cairns, numerous hut circles and a very large causewayed enclosure). The Burren is for many still an intensely personal landscape.

1. Karen Walls The Quest for the Celtic Keys 2014 (kindle version only available). ISBN 978-1-990912-43-4
2. Jackie Queally Spirit of the Burren 2013 ISBN 978-0-9541435-9-6
3. Freddy Silva The Divine Blueprint 2102

Temple Cronan cell church with reliquary in foreground.

Chapter One
WATER

I would like to begin now with the element of water. Water energetically boosts the electro- magnetic energies present in rocks. Humans, animals and birds can sense these energies and are affected by them in a positive or negative way depending on their tolerance range. The Burren limestone hills do not carry rivers above ground as the water find the quickest way underground through the numerous cracks in the soluble rock. Limestone has a high silica content known to enhance meditation and higher consciousness. The mass of rushing water below the surface boosts the energies of the land expanse, by enhancing these electro magnetic frequencies inherent in the rock. The positive effect of negative ions that the underground waters emit are beneficial for human and animal health, as evidenced in the health of the cattle and goats that roam the hills. It is not surprising that people visiting the Burren remark on how they feel energised or expansive there.

The area around Gort lies to the east of the Burren Hills, in what has recently been coined by a new term: the Burren Lowlands. Predominantly limestone, it is a very special area — geologically it is unique by world standards. The limestone is older here than in the Burren hills, for the limestone has been eroded by constant rain to create a pleasant rolling terrain, through which rivers weave their way above and below the rock. The river that enters Gort Town changes its name in numerous sections of its journey as it dips and dives and rises again. In the Gort Lowlands where caves and often rushing rivers are both below and above the ground there can be quite an unsettling effect on an energetic level! Its constant changing energy is akin to the persona of a trickster — and the folk tales of the region collected by Lady Gregory and others last century testify to this being an intensely fairy-like region. The topography and waters conspire to create this effect. Fields and roads can be flooded for months in times of heavy rain, and then as the water disappears, the lakes or 'turloughs' retreat. Plants have to adapt to their temporary drownings. This elemental, watery region belongs to the dreamtime. It is as if it is saying: "Nothing is as it seems!" One of my favourite spots is the underground cave outside of Gort known as Caenahowan. It is a wonderful place to stand when there is a Full Moon. The river emerges from this deep cave only to disappear further downstream again at another swallow hole.

Avian spirit in water at Caenahowan.

Water

In the lee of the Burren Mountains, in the parish of Beagh in the southern extremity of County Galway, farmers have done a great job in restoring many of the holy wells. Sometimes farmers who can dowse for water also develop a great interest in dowsing leylines. Tony Diviney near Gort engraved the pattern of leys on a capstone over the well he dowsed. Wells are an intrinsic part of the early Christian fabric of the region, and were no doubt Pagan sites of worship before the Christians came along.

There are many holy wells in the Burren, ranging from large areas such as St Columba's Well at Columkille, where the water tumbles through the walls in winter and rushes past the tree-ridden fulacht fia (burnt mounds — an archaeological term) into basins in the bowl-like arena

Carving of leys emanating from central triskele above well in Beagh Parish

Water

St Cronan's Well below cliffs at St Cronan's, Carron

Standing stone besides St Cronan's Well.

below, to small ones like St Cronans near Carron where a standing stone still remains on top of the small mound beside a holy well, found tucked in a cleft below the cliff.

The most famous holy well is that of St Brigid in Liscannor not far off the Cliffs of Moher. Unsurprisingly it lays on strong leylines. Holy wells or springs positioned on leys

St. Columkille's Well, near Carron.

boost the magnetic frequencies of the telluric energies of the land. One can trace the course of the spring from the back of the cemetery through to the roadside and follow its onward course below the land. St Brigid was the female counterpart to the god Lugh, and to Lon the Smith mentioned later. She is the patron saint of healing, poetry and smithing.

Water

St. Brigid's Well entrance.

Interestingly, folk used to visit the well on Lughnasa — which became known as Garland Sunday in Christian times, when it was the only public holiday in the year for the labouring population. Aside from Christmas Day, this date bore great local significance, and there are further references to Lugh in the sandhills of Liscannor.

Water

Waterfall at St. Brigid's Well.

Cliffs of Moher from land.

Water

*Cliffs of Moher from sea.
Kevin Lynch.*

Chapter Two
WOOD

Moving onto the Wood element that the Water feeds, Wood belongs to the domain of high morals, initiating change and high confidence as typified by the early saints with their lone retreats among the rocks. They often came to the Burren from the Aran Islands which housed so many of these early Christians, e.g. Enda, Macdara, Colman.

These early monks, or Culdees, set themselves apart attitudinally from the later Roman Church. The group consisted of both men and women, whose pure intent was to serve God in devotional, mystical and practical ways. They practised healing by way of service to the local communities they lived in. The oral tradition says that whenever they reached twelve in number they split into another group that formed a new settlement. Often they were on the move with their bell. Wherever they stopped they would ring their bell and say a simple Mass for those who gathered. For their stopping points they used the old sacred sites such as sacred trees, standing stones, natural mounds and wells. It is very difficult to date the start of the Culdees, although Roman and Greek travel writers record their presence in Britain as early as 37 AD, and it is very likely the Culdees were here in Ireland too, having crossed the sea in coracles, their simple waterproof boats. In recent decades there has been a revival of interest in these early Christians, with the belief growing that they escaped from Jerusalem when the Roman governor occupied the city and dispelled many religious sects. They fled into the south of France and even onwards

Mound close to Carron Church

to Britain and Ireland. Some sites in the Burren that stem from the early Medieval period hint at a continuation of their early non-Roman Christian ideology.

It is an ideology that twinned the native pagan faith with the new one that was concerned with the Christ energy. For instance at Carron Church deep in the Burren there was the custom of bearing the coffin thrice around the ancient cairn close by the church before burying the body.

In Kilnaboy a Cross of Lorraine incorporated in the stonework at the western gable end reminds me of where I saw this same symbol carved on a medieval boundary stone in West Lothian in Scotland, in what was once territory belonging to the Knights Templar (at nearby Torphicen

Preceptory a stone testifies that they officially fused with the Knights of St John around the time of the Reformation!).

The Knights Templars are somewhat of an enigma in Ireland. In Scotland often they established themselves in the same region where the early Christians/Culdees dwelt. In Ireland the Templars settled in small settlements in the south east, in south Cork, on the Shannon estuary in Limerick, in Galway City and in County Sligo, sailing along the rivers and coastline. I have wondered at times if they also came to the Burren.

Certainly the monastic complex of Kilmacduagh has an early church from their times dedicated to one of their chief saints John the Baptist, and that monastery was of regional import then. In any case, at Kilnaboy the cross of Lorraine is an enigma. Often connected with the Crusades, the symbol could mean that some Crusaders, or even Templars, passed through. Kilnaboy also has its own sheela-na-gig, an Irish character in stone. The carving is placed over the doorway and shows a female figure exposing her genitalia, as all sheela-na-gigs do!!

One of my favourite churches sports an alleged inverted sheela-na-gig besides its window. Beyond Corofin the ancient church of Raha overlooks the mysterious lake where a Brock Shee (fairy badger) was successfully dispelled by St Blathmaic there.

Returning to Kilnaboy Parish, it has a unique stone

Wood

Sheela-na-Gig above arch at Kilnaboy Church.

Close-up comparison of Sheela-na-Gig at Aughagower, Co Mayo.

Wood

Tau Cross replica stone (original in Local museum, Corofin)

presumed to mark either a parish boundary or a pilgrimage route to Kilfenora Cathedral. This marker may have been taller than what remains now. The stone depicts a Tau cross. Its remarkable double head either end of the T-shape is also a very sacred symbol, hinting at a place of great reverence and power.

The core energy of the Burren lends itself well to the lone retreater. My favourite hermitage is one that appeals to many visitors and locals alike. It is St Colman's Hermitage under Eagles Rock near Kinvara. This hermitage was until recent years completely overgrown with scrub and trees. Here is a picture of the offerings left recently on a simple stone slab that used to act as an altar there. Nearby a simple altar slab was placed over the water as it gathers at the well. When altars were placed over water veins in the earth, the intent would have been to align the prayers with the power of the waters in order to boost their efficacy. What sets the Burren and the Aran Islands apart is the large number of hermitages, in addition to possible early Christian settlements. These Atlantic islands and the Burren (which encompasses the Burren Lowlands too) are places set apart. I feel it is such places that humanity needs to visit in these times of chaos and lack of perspective. The region clears the head and even allows you to dream new thoughts into existence.

Wood

Offerings on altar at St Colman's Retreat.

Hermit's Cave under Eagles Rock, Slieve Carran.

Wood

Chapter Three
FIRE

Now wood feeds the fire, an element that is often somewhat hidden, only occasionally erupting in most people. Similarly in the land there are intermittent volcanoes that thankfully are not an everyday occurrence! I sought out dragon myths in the vicinity of the Burren, since dragons are closely related to the fire element. I also associate fire with passion and adventure, and in relation to this aspect I can mention some local myths in which mythical heroes exhibit their fiery natures. The greatest myth I know of is that of Lon the Smith.

Long before Ireland became a Celtic nation in popular history, its mythical history speaks of a race of people who merged with the fairy kingdom as their rule drew to a close. This was the de Danaan who descended from the goddess Danu. When the Milesians invaded and the likes of Finn McCool began their takeover battles, these peaceful people slipped into the caves and caverns deep underground where they continued their rule. A possible date for this is circa 2000BC after the Battle of Tailte.

During their invasion, in an isolated pocket of fertility in wilds of the Burren, Lon the Smith lived on. He still carried that spark of magic associated with these "fairy folk". He was a smith who worked the element of fire: a very important occupation within a tribe in those days. His anvil was created from a third arm that protruded from his chest, and perhaps to make up for it he only had one leg, upon which he could bound long distances when he needed to. Lon lived in a smithy cave (no longer identifiable) in the townland of Teeskagh, and cinders lined the floor of his underground home. Perhaps the cave still exists in another dimension. Lon fashioned weapons and other metal objects and was able to rely on his magical cow to produce copious milk. His cow Glasha grazed on the nearby mountain of Slieve na Glasha. This cow gave so much milk that no vessel was able to contain it all. Every day one of Lon's seven sons tended his precious cow, and every night they would turn her round by the tail to face her bed where she lay — and to this day no blade of grass will grow there. Lon had stolen Glasha from Spain — the land where the incoming Milesians came from. One day two women approached him with a request to milk his cow, and one of these women deceived him by bringing along a milking pail in which she had bored several holes. As the milk flowed through the pail it reached the ground and created streams that flowed down over the nearby escarpment, creating seven waterfalls. These are known as the Seven Streams of the Overflowing and can be viewed in winter when rainfall is higher and the hazel scrub has died away.

Meanwhile Lon had heard that the famous warrior Finn McCool had landed on the East side of Ireland near where Dublin now stands, and he set off in leaps and bounds to meet him. In next to no time he was there to declare his profession to his new ruler. He also lay a gesa, which is a challenge that one is obliged to follow up if personally delivered. He challenged anyone to overtake him on the

Fire

way home. Caoilte from Finn's band of warriors managed to reach Lon's home first, swiftly followed by Lon himself who warmly welcomed him into his home. He confessed the gesa had been a mere ruse to entice the warriors over. He now set about fashioning them their own swords. At the end of three days Lon had created swords for all seven of Finn's warriors and also for Finn himself. Testing the strength of their swords on Lon's anvil (which presumably was his own arm!) they easily broke it. Then they set out to destroy all the warrior De Danaans who were guarding the causeways that led to Teeskagh, that green and beautiful hill. The unfortunate De Danaanites were cut to pieces and the earthbound Lon was forced henceforth to live as a mortal, eking out a living from his smith craft. It is also said that someone from Ulster stole his cow shortly after that too. If you go to Slieve na Glasha and spend time wandering round on top looking for the bare patches where the magical cow lay, you will probably absorb the timeless atmosphere of this hill.

This tale tells of the fiery nature by which cultures are taken over wholesale by new races. There are many cosmological components to the mystical tale, for the cow of plenty is associated with the female divine energies in the Milky Way. In mystical faery lore, the Milky Way represents the Under realm! In the tale, the seven sons under the instructions of their wizard father protect his sacred cow who seems to represent the old female consciousness. They yield to the new masculine consciousness of the seven warriors, overseen by their mighty chieftain father Finn Mc Cool.

Fire

The stark changeover also mirrors the shift that is occurring astronomically in our sky as a great transit of stars within the Milky Way undergoes a 245 year great shift, heralding a new consciousness that is seeding once more.

The other aspect of Fire that has to be acknowledged in the Burren area lies in the Dragon myths that creep in from time to time. At Kilshanny near Ennistymon stands a massive cairn on the banks of the Daly (Irish: Daelach) river known as Cairn Connaughton/ Connaughtu. When I first approached it, having gained permission from the farmer, it pulsated as I drew near. I could feel its tremendous presence in my bones and in my heart. One tale tells of a northern army from Connaught chasing a big serpent up from Corcomroe to this cairn, whereupon they slew it and buried it inside.

Serpents or dragons are synonymous in myth with deep earth energies that connect with the fire in your belly or your heart. When it is buried in such a fashion it is really marking the spot where the earth energies are harvested and stored. Small wonder then I felt its presence some yards off! It is interesting that the dragon energy seemed to shift from Corcomroe to here — perhaps the tale reflects a parallel shift that took place in religious life in the latter half of the twelfth century. The Roman Church introduced a new ideology at Corcomroe Abbey, which was quite unlike that of the earlier school of monks who lived in harmony with nature, respectful of the old ways. Close to the giant cairn lay an Augustinian abbey at Kilshanny. This order was

Cairn Connaughton, Kilshanny near Ennistymon. Kevin Lynch.

typically more concerned with papal theology than practical farming affairs. Also in the Ennistymon area lies the church of St MacCreehy, who banished a dragon in Liscannor Bay besides the church. There is a bestial carving showing him devouring human bones in the church. Apparently there were more carvings that have been removed over the passage of time. Cat-like monsters are another symbol for earth energies, particularly leylines. St Senan came face to face with Catach the dragon after the archangel Michael transported him to Scattery Island. Senan slew Catach and slung him into Doo Lough below the holy mountain, Slieve Callan, on the mainland towards Milltown Malbay. Dragon temples occur at Scattery Island further south where the Shannon meets the sea, on Inismaan in the Aran Isles offshore and at Loop Head in west Clare, according to

Fire

Carving of dragon at St MacCreehy's church ruins.

popular novelist John Windele in 1750. On Scattery Island stood a very tall round tower, and in the diametrically opposed northeast of the Burren a similar one stands in full height, known as Kilmacduagh. Round towers act like acupuncture points that harness the earth energies at certain spots, a process that the capture and slaying of fiery dragons at sites describe in veiled terms. Dragon energies are deeply rooted to our subconscious. I often sensed that the area round Liscannor carries with it a far older consciousness that has a clear connection to the magic of the earth.

My grandmother from Miltown Malbay married a farmer on the coast road there, and was a renowned storyteller when alive. She was full of wisdom and generosity of spirit. Her

Fire

outlook and whole psyche seemed to me cyclical rather than linear, aside from when cruelly forced into a linear timeline whenever she bade farewell to her emmigrant children. The gentle ways of the old Clare people do not immediately remind one of the element of fire, though I would maintain it surfaces in the deep passion the people hold for the land they live in. One can certainly sense fire in the mythical tales of fiery heroes like Diarmid and Grainne as they fled from Finn MacCool, hiding in fairy forts and under dolmens until eventually they reached the Oughtdara valley near Doolin where they settled. Oughtdara is a veritable fairy glen. It brings us neatly to the next element which is Earth, as epitomised by the fairy palace deep within the Hill of Health here in Oughtdara in the west of Ireland.

Fire

Chapter Four
EARTH

I first came across Oughtdara, inland from Doolin, when attending a ceremony specially devised by a progressiveminded priest to ask forgiveness for burying young children in a killeen (a killeen is a collection of unmarked graves set in an isolated spot outside of a Christian graveyard). This was common practice up until recent decades in Ireland. How fitting that this killeen was placed in the lee of one of Ireland's chief fairy sites. The legend goes that when Finn lost his wife Grainne to Diarmid he gave chase, always consulting his oracular thumb by placing it in his mouth, for that action gave him the power to see exactly where they were, and he could set his hounds on them. He lost his favourite hound in the chase. Seefin is buried above Black Head under a cairn by that name. Finn was unable to find the couple because they hid under a dolmen (a table-shaped monument) and then heaped seaweed over it so as to disguise their hiding place. Finn assumed they were drowned when he saw the pile of seaweed so ended his search! Just a little south of their last outpost stands a fort atop a distinct conical mound. Conical shaped hills often have special roles to play in the landscape. This hill in Oughtdara is known as the Hill of Health and is said to be the chief residence of the Sidhe in Ireland. When you approach it from the killeen you really can sense an otherworldliness to this place. I walked in this hidden vale and felt transported, even though I knew nothing then about its strong fairy associations. I took several photos of the Hill of Health and all of them came out in an unusual mode compared to others elsewhere that day, which came out looking normal.

Fairy Hill, Oughtdara, taken by colleague on one occasion

same Fairy Hill of Heath in an altered dimension perceived by me

Often when I sense another dimension in a local landscape and take a picture with a camera the result seems to reflect that subtle change in energies, as illustrated by the second photograph, which imparts a dream-like quality. It may

Earth

well be a place of fairy energies. Fairies reside where the earth energies are generally strong and enchanting. In the old days people in Ireland used to regularly sight them, but nowadays many have lost their belief in them and so they do not see them. One has to believe in something for it to manifest, and as mystics remind us, form always follows thought. Imagination had a key role to play in the successful sighting of fairies. Imagination is the essential quality. After all, it is imagination that inspires the best inventors to this day!

It well worth visiting this mythical landscape and soaking up its rare energies. An early saint sought out this rarified spot for reflection and prayer — St Macdara had his cell church here. A serpent carved on its walls has sadly long

Dragon in tree.

gone. (This saint also resided on the isle of Macdara off the Connemara coast where there an enchanting cell church and unusual cross slabs remain. The old ring forts that housed small clans of extended families clans are long associated with the fairies still, and sometimes carry fascinating fairy lore with them. One of my favourite ring forts lies off the beaten track on Loch Avalla Farm in the Burren National Park (near Gortlecka past Mullaghmor).

My favourite fairy fort on Lough Avalla Farm

There is a tree growing within this fort that has spurred a dramatic-looking dragon face in one of its long twisted branches (see p.35). Often such shapes are shaped by the nature beings to reflect the energies of the place. A blackthorn and a hawthorn grow intertwined there, and it is hard to see where one starts and the other ends. It is a truly magical place to sit in and experience the joyous vibrations this hidden ring fort emits. An area often overlooked that is strong in earth energies is the region of the eastern Burren, centred on Gort.

I mentioned in the Water section of this book the unorthodox flow patterns that intertwine with the turloughs. The water serves to emphasise the magical qualities — you could say it affects the folk psyche of the area. It would have been a strong contributing factor in why Lady Gregory was able to gather so much folklore and fairy tales from the region when she lived at Coole Park about a hundred years ago. Her house has long gone but remnants of the estate remain.

Steps at Coole.

The energy of locality often expresses itself in fairy tales, and perhaps contributes a vital ingredient in their lasting success as a story form. Chanting and vocal toning can assist humans in connecting with fairy places that carry unusual frequencies. Often people see flitting colours or hear faint music in such places — it awakens unusual sensations. It is not necessary to see fairies with wings on them to understand that the veil is thin in such places.

On Slieve Elva once I was drawn to a grove of hawthorn that grew away from the mountain track. I did not know at the time that Ireland's longest underground river passed through here. I took a photograph as I stood between the two main trees in its centre. It came out as a vortex of energy. Something prompted me to take another photograph just a few steps back from the centre and this one came out normal. I toyed with the meaning of the name Elva as it reminded me of elves. In fact it also interested me that a strong leyline passes through Slieve Elva on its way to the Norwegian town of Aldval - this means Valley of the Elves! I will discuss this in the Metal section that follows now, for the Earth feeds the Metal element.

Earth

Fairy Hawthorn Grove.

Earth

Chapter Five
METAL

I have mentioned leys several times in this small book. Leys are lines, not normally visible on the surface of the earth, which emit a subtle energy field that can be detected using dowsing rods, or by using your own hands if sensitive enough. Some people have the ability to see these lines as streams of light beaming across the land. I have met such people in Ireland, and have witnessed how other cultures rely on these sightings to inform them where to build their monasteries or temples, even to this day. The knowledge of leylines belongs to the field of geomancy, which in the Middle Ages in Europe was used extensively for siting churches, while earlier still, no doubt, sites were chosen in this way for important forts and ceremonial sites.

Late in 2008 I received an "earth grid" from Anthony Peart, a geomancer living in Lincolnshire England. (1) An earth grid is a complex of leylines forming a pattern often based on mathematical laws of " sacred geometry". His grid revealed a beautiful and intricate pattern of leylines in the Burren. One leyline in the local grid runs parallel to the Cliffs of Moher, which now attracts so many visitors. It extends into the holy well of St Brigit down the hill. Wells serve to boost the magnetic properties of these lines. There are many interesting observations I could make regarding this Burren grid. For instance I can see that many hermitages and monasteries are sited on extending lines of its main pentagram. Often these mysterious earth grids link in a cog-like manner with others elsewhere, like invisible fingers

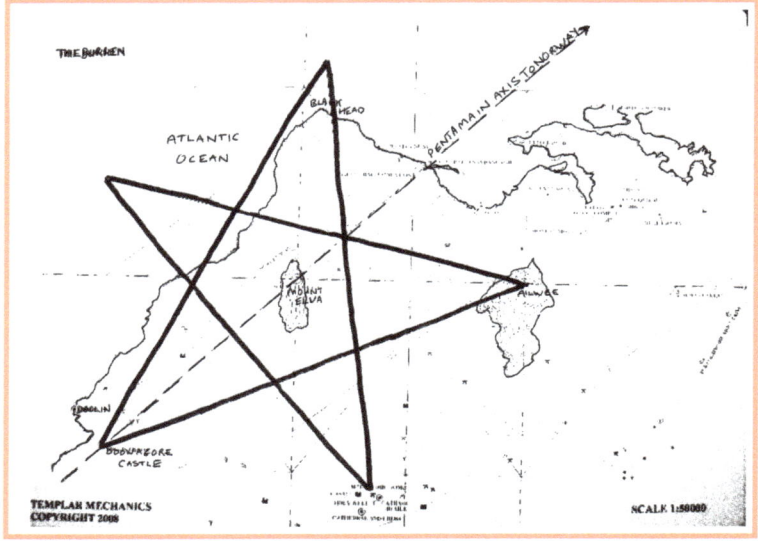

Pentagram showing main ley from Doonagore Castle near Doolin

reaching across the globe. For instance, the central axis of the pentagram leads from the fairy-tale looking castle of Doonagore by Doolin to the holy mountain Trondfjell above Aldval in Norway--the mountain is shaped like a throne and was a major stopping point on a medieval pilgrimage route.

The leys often attract resonant external events along their axis. In the case of the pentagram, a Norweigan local author was living on the slopes of Trondfjell for many years, and wrote a book entitled The Norwegian Pentagram. In his historical investigation he traced the same pentagonal pattern as exists in the Burren, albeit on a grander scale! Harald Boehlke believes that fleeing Irish monks were instrumental in marking out this pattern, which came about when the sites were chosen for building the first cathedrals in Norway - dependant upon the monks' intricate knowledge of masonry.

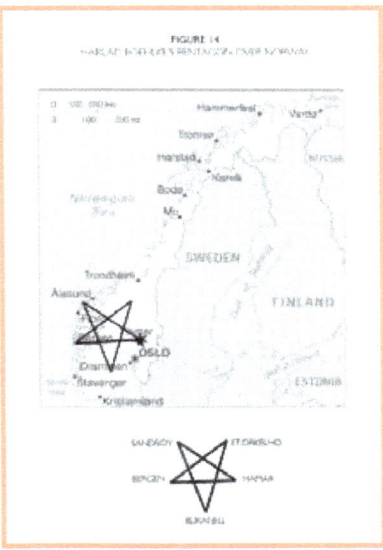

Norway pentagram.

Within hours of receiving the map of the Burren earth grid, I heard from Eddie Stack, an Irish writer who was researching Doolin for a book he was writing. He told me of a medieval immram called the Maeldun Saga (immrams are Irish ecclesiastical teaching aids written in the form of Irish travel fantasia). Eddie Stack told me that he believes the monks in that tale actually set off from Doolin, near the Cliffs of Moher, around the same period that Harald Boehlke's research revealed that Irish monks were landing in Norway. Eddie always thought the islands in the immram were located in Norway! If so, the monks were leaving behind an area with a pentagram grid encoded in the land,

and travelling to a new country where a macrocosmic pentagram grid lay..

The east-west axis in the grid extends into the sea and cuts between the Aran islands of Iniseer and Inismaan. This axis also traverses the two main mountains in the Burren.

Cliffs of Moher. Kevin Lynch..

The mountains of Slieve Elva and Slieve Ailwee in effect form the centres of two major overlapping circles in the earth grid. Both mountains have underground river courses running through them — Ireland's longest underground river makes for spectacular caving under Elva, while the longest dry river cave in Ireland is open to the public under Ailwee Mountain.

I have travelled with visitors in the Burren who have had

spiritual awakenings on the leys, and I have met local people who have in some way or other tuned into the key spots on the leylines, and created artefacts that mirror the quality of the earth grid.

Doonagore.

The topic of earth grids is really too vast for this booklet to do it justice, but I am available for short presentations if interested, or you may read more on it in my book Spirit of the Burren.

The local earth grid featuring the pentagram links with another more esoteric grid system that resonates with the Metatronic energies overseen by archangel Metatron, whose chief agent is Archangel Michael. These grids are recognized by retired Naval commander William Buehler who has dedicated many years to studying them world-

Metal

wide. He maintains that the Burren carries with it a very high chakra energy system capable of working with very divine beings. Its resonant divine energies would attract present seekers and past hermits alike. The Burren appears to be divinely protected, thus allowing it to remain an area that is pristine and relatively unspoilt. Above all it carries the pure Christic ray that surely influenced the poetry and writings of John O'Donohue deceased (2008). John came from the Caher Valley above Fanore and eloquently expressed in works such as Anam Cara how he understood the power of nature to move the soul. I view John as the embodiment of the strong ancestral energies that the Burren holds.

One phenomenon peculiar to Irish early Christian monasteries is the round tower. These vary in height ,as does the level of the doorway above the ground. On Scattery Island in the mouth of the Shannon southwest of the Burren there is a round tower in ruins whose doorway is level with the ground — this island has many old churches on it and was regarded as a very holy island.

On the opposite northeast side of the Burren at Kilmacduagh stands Ireland's tallest extant round tower at just over 111 feet. Its doorway is 26 feet off the ground and seems to face the holy isle of Lindisfarne off Northumberland when plotted using GPS. The limestone from the Burren consists of egg-like particles of compressed, decomposed sea creatures. The tower is built with this local limestone, a more magnetic stone than the normal limestone that traditional houses were built with.

Metal

Kilmacduagh Round Tower.

Professor Callahan researched the 'diamagnetic' and 'paramagnetic' properties that work together in the presence of round towers. As a trained entomologist he did much research on the raison d'être for the erection of these towers, and he concluded that if the subtle electromagnetic energies were already balanced the doorway did not have to be raised — often they were raised a good deal above ground level, and at times quartz-filled rubble was placed in the cavity of the bottom layers of the wall in order to tweak its conductivity. Callahan likens the action of the round towers to the way that insects can use their antennae to find nectar.

He says that the towers work with solar energies to both store and emit beneficial paramagnetic particles into the soil and air, which in turn helps with local fertility of the soil. It also disperses rare solar rays into the environment at large.

This remarkable tower is said to have been built by the Goban Saor, an exceptionally wise and witty wandering mason quasi-architect. He was a contemporary of St Macduagh in the seventh century and is said to have come from Ferns Abbey in Co Wexford at Macduagh's bidding.

The story of how St Macduagh founded the monastery at Kilmacduagh is interesting, for he abandoned his hidden hermitage when his long lost cousin, the chieftain King Guaire, gave him permission to choose a site upon which to build a monastery.

As Macduagh walked the land he stopped at many wells that bear his name to this day, and he waited for the sign an angel had told him would be given. When his girdle broke loose and fell on the ground he knew this was the spot upon which to build his monastery. Could it be that this site is on a sacral chakra point on a local leyline, as the girdle lies across the sacral chakra on the body?

In spiritual terms one of the main tasks of the sacral centre is to distribute the vital energy of the sun force (which Professor Callahan maintains is the role of round towers!). In Hindu spirituality there are six streams to this vital energy and a seventh that goes directly to the centre. If

St. Colmans well near Kilmacduagh.

you count the windows round the rim of the round tower there are six evenly spaced windows. Perhaps they stream out the cosmic forces..certainly this degree of regularity in the placing of the windows is unusual in round towers and suggested an intent behind the design. Perhaps the round tower itself represents Number 7, since it is surrounded by the six windows. The central tower incidentally contained six wooden floors too.

I believe that these round towers originally were built to aid prayer and meditation rather than as a defence mechanism. I entered one in Scotland and was able to dowse the strong energies, and one international teacher of spiritual healing remarked to me how the floors equated with the chakra centres in a vertical line - thus they would have been an excellent teaching aid for the monks who may well have meditated on each floor. Moreover, at the time these round towers were built the Christianity practised was more aligned with the early Jerusalem church and true spiritual power, rather than the Roman style which sought to create a hierarchal structure to a religion aligned with temporal power. Kilmacduagh was the hub of a complex of small abbot-led establishments who followed a non-hierarchal humble tradition, serving God and Nature, his goddess consort. There were earlier, even smaller, older monasteries in the region, all long disappeared. The glorious round tower at Kilmacduagh still stands testimony to those times and is a fitting end to our cycle.

There is much more I could say about this tower, following similar lines of investigation that this book has been indicating. There is much more to say about the Burren too, but this booklet is only a taster.

In short the Burren has a very large and beautiful spirit

Metal

that encompasses very high vibrational energies. There is a series of subtle and extremely high chakras here that man rarely encounters on Earth. The energies reach into the angelic realms and correspondingly activate energies from the inner Earth sphere to which the fairy spirits respond with great love and joy.

You may read more in-depth matter about the Burren area in her book Spirit of the Burren. Even better, why not leave the everyday world behind and engage with the natural energies of the Burren and its unique lowlands? Choose from either a short day tour or a longer sojourn/ retreat.

You may practise dowsing, simple "Gaia" Touch exercises, and toning with your voices in order to connect deeper with nature and the essence of the Burren. Gong and tuning forks are useful tools we also use to connect with the Earth.

Please contact jackiequeally@gmail.com in the first instance. She is available for presentations and workshops on topics such as earth grids, sacred landscapes and the five elements, and dowsing. The full range of services available for helping you rekindle the connection between yourself and the blessed Earth are at

www.earthwise.me or
www.spirit-of-burren.com

Notes

Notes

Notes

www.ingramcontent.com/pod-product-compliance
Ingram Content Group UK Ltd.
Pitfield, Milton Keynes, MK11 3LW, UK
UKHW020243240426
12048UKWH00026B/1579